HEATHROW CYBER SERVICES NIG LIMITED

www.heathrowtrainingservices.com

PRODUCTS AND SERVICES BOOK

HEATHROW HOUSE, C/O 24 Kigoma Street Wuse, Zone 7, FCT, Abuja, Tel: +2347063971477, RC 918214,
joshuajogo@hotmail.com
www.heathrowtrainingservices.com

HEATHROW CYBER SERVICES IS A SISTER COMPANY OF HEATHROW TRAINING SERVICES UK
ALL RIGHTS RESERVED. COPYRIGHT MATERIAL.

MESSAGE FROM THE CEO

As a response to the express invitation by His Excellency, President Mohammadu Buhari to Nigerians in diaspora to come home and help in his transformation agenda for the country, the board of directors of Heathrow Training Services UK directed that an international liaison office be opened in Abuja for this purpose. This eventually led to the establishment of a sister company, Heathrow Cyber Services Nig Ltd. This subsidiary company has been established to help in the president's transformation agenda in the areas of ICT training, technology acquisition, project management training, political innovation and strategy. The purpose of this booklet is to bring to you our range of products and services available in Nigeria pursuant to the transformation agenda. For real and lasting transformation to be implemented in Nigeria, adequate training and education of the populace is highly desirable and must be the bedrock of any successful transformation agenda. For the president's transformation vision to succeed and be sustained, essential training and education must be the blue print for success. It is to this regard that HCS wants to be a strategic partner in progress.

We want to focus attention on the acquisition of best practice project management skills. Project Manager and Best Practice Training including Prince2 aimed at Project Managers and IT Technical Staff wanting to get into Project Management.

Our key target is to get majority of Nigerian youths ICT certified and to produce in every sector of the Nigerian Economy qualified project managers. Today Nigeria has the un-enviable record of having the highest number of abandoned projects in the world. Training qualified Prince2 project Managers within the country becomes desirable in sustaining economic growth. To achieve this we are making IT certification and Prince2 trainings available throughout the nooks and crannies of Nigeria through our popular mobile cyber institute. "You don't have to go to school anymore, our school comes to you"!

Joshua Jogo
CEO
The Heathrow Group Uk
joshuajogo@hotmail.com

INTRODUCTION

Heathrow Cyber Services is the Nigeria based offering of Heathrow Training Services UK, a cutting edge training and educational resources company. Our strategic alliances with key training companies in the UK have provided the unique platform to facilitate numerous courses with many experienced and qualified facilitators.

We are able to provide custom made training to suit the needs and requirements of any establishment. This can be done in conjunction with our consultants.

We also have a repertoire of capacity building courses which will help to transform the different levels of management to a 21st century ready team with measurable competitive advantage. An example is PRINCE2, a UK government written course recognised and used worldwide as the best practice in projects management. We are the authorized training organisation (ATO) for PRINCE2 in Nigeria.

We are able to organise training both locally and internationally at our prestigious training centres in the UK, South Africa, USA, and Nigeria. We can also deploy online training where needed for a particular department or group of departments.

About Us

Heathrow Cyber Services Nig Ltd is a Training Provider that offers high level self-study and blended instructor led learning solutions for corporate, government and individual users. We are based in the UK and have offices in South Africa, Australia and Nigeria. In addition, we offer consultancy and executive recruitment services.

Heathrow Cyber Services Nig Ltd is part of the Heathrow Group which consists of the following businesses:

Heathrow Publishing and Marketing UK
Heathrow Mobile Cyber Institute UK
Heathrow Consultancy Services UK
Heathrow Cyber Security Services UK
Heathrow Gateway International Centre (NGO)

Vision

To provide products and services in ICT and Technology in furtherance of the Millennium development Goals.

1. Provide training in specialist ICT skills and certifications
2. Promote technical skills acquisition and certifications
3. provide office and business related skills
4. provide services in technological acquisition and implementation
5. provide training in political innovation and strategy
6. Provide mass computer literacy training throughout the country with a strategic vision to make at least 80% of the Nigerian population computer literate by 2020.
7. Put a computer in every Nigerian home by 2020.
8. Provide high level ICT and Cyber Security Services second to none in the country

BELOW ARE OUR PRODUCTS AND SERVICES

1. THE PRINCE2 AND PRINCE2 MASTER CLASS

What is PRINCE2?

PRINCE2 is the world's leading **project management course** - helping you use logical and organised stages, defined steps and clearly identified roles, responsibilities and relationships to deliver tangible benefits.

More than 4,000 people experience PRINCE2 courses and PRINCE2 training every month in the UK alone, confident in the knowledge that the methodology encourages a best practice approach to running projects in a consistent framework.

Since its introduction PRINCE2 has become the de facto standard for project management in both the public and private sectors.

Until now, PRINCE2 training courses were only available in the UK. But now we are able to offer you this widely respected training course right here in Nigeria. This is made possible by the recently signed strategic partnership between NetPost Nigeria Ltd, an associate company of NIPOST and Heathrow Cyber Services Nig Ltd, a sister company of Heathrow Training Services Ltd UK.

Thousands of UK professionals have successfully used PRINCE2 courses to create a standard and structured approach to their project management, running projects which are well-organised, well-planned and results-driven, we believe that the same record can be achieved here in Nigeria.

And, because PRINCE2 is an easily-tailored solution which can be used in any environment and divides projects into manageable stages, it ensures the efficient control and use of resources and regular process monitoring.

When used effectively, PRINCE2 training ensures that successful projects have:

- A planned, organised and controlled start, middle and end
- Regular reviews of progress against the plan and the business case
- Flexible decision points
- Automatic management control of deviations from the plan
- Stakeholder and management involvement at the right time and place
- Excellent communication channels between the project, project management and the rest of the organisation

PRINCE2®

Foundation & Practitioner

Officially launched in October 1996, PRINCE2® is the method used for planning and managing projects in the public and private sectors. The method is used for a wide variety and size of projects. PRINCE2® is universally accepted as best practice project management.

Who Should Study
All organisations, government departments, public servants, company executives, and individuals requiring a controlled approach to managing projects.
The PRINCE2® method is flexible and adaptable for any type and size of project, and offers an excellent management foundation for any member of staff.

TARGET AUDIENCE
This course would benefit:
- Project & Programme Managers
- Directors and General Managers

- Team Managers and support staff
- Staff who will have a defined role
- Project Management Consultants

Course objectives
The key objectives of this course are:
Understand the PRINCE2 method at the Foundation and, where chosen, the Practitioner levels.
Understand how to apply the integrated elements of PRINCE2 (principles, processes, themes and tailoring) within a work environment.
Understand the benefits and principles underlying a structured approach to project management.
Help delegates to operate effectively with colleagues and managers within a structured project management environment.

Course Approach
Heathrow Cyber Services Nig Ltd in partnership with NetPost are now able to offer Prnce2 as an E-learning training course with your own personal tutor and training online and offline with DVD supplied. The good news too is that now students are able to access the course materials for longer instead of the traditional 3 days or 5 days workshop. Student can have up to six months access giving them more flexibility of time and preparation in order to achieve a high pass mark at the Prince2 Exams.

Examinations
Foundation: 1 hour, closed book exam consisting of 75 multiple-choice questions

5 questions to be trail and not counted in scores

35 marks required (out of 70 available) to pass – 50%

Practitioner: 2½ hours, open book (PRINCE2® manual only) consisting of 9 scenario based objective test questions with 12 marks available per question. All question items will be worth 1 mark, making the total number of marks available 108

The pass mark is 55%. Candidates will need to achieve at least 59 out of the 108 to pass the examination.

To maintain your Practitioner Qualification you will need to sit and pass a Re-Registration exam within 5 years of passing your original examination
Practitioner Re-Registration: open book (PRINCE2® manual only) consisting of 3 scenario-based objective test questions.

Course Content

- **Structured Approach to Managing Projects** Setting the scene for a structured approach to managing all projects; project success criteria; the model of the PRINCE2 method including the integrated elements of principles, processes, themes and tailoring. - **The Process-based Approach** PRINCE2 focuses on key processes needed for successful project management which must be present, but may be 'tailored' to reflect the complexity, scope and risks faced by the project. SPOCE's PRINCE2 Process Model will be used to help delegates understand and appreciate what should be done to manage each project, why it should be done and when in the project lifecycle. - **Business Case** What is a Business Case; Outcomes, Outputs, Benefits and	- **Progress** Management and Technical Stages. Tolerance and Raising Exceptions. Project Board and Project Manager Controls for Reviewing and Reporting Progress; Baselines for Control; Capturing and Reporting Lessons; Event-driven and time-driven controls; Progress Responsibilities. - **Change** Issue and Change Control procedure; Configuration Management procedure; Configuration Management Strategy; Baselining, handling changes to, tracking and protecting products. Change Authority and Change Budget; Change Responsibilities. - **Quality** Quality Defined, The Quality Audit Trial; Quality; Acceptance Criteria, Quality Criteria, Quality Management Strategy, Quality Assurance, Quality

Dis-benefits; Developing, Verifying and Maintaining the Business Case; Contents of the Business Case; Confirming the benefits and the Benefits Review Plan; Business Case Responsibilities. • **Organisation** Project Management Team Structure and the Project Board, Project Assurance, Project Manager, Team Manager, Change Authority and Project Support roles & responsibilities. Stakeholder management; Communication Management Strategy; Organization Responsibilities. • **Plans** Levels and content of Plans; Exception Plans; Product-based approach to planning – Project Product Description, Product Breakdown Structure, Product Description, Product Flow Diagram; the PRINCE2 planning steps; Plans Responsibilities. •	Controls and Quality Review technique; Quality Responsibilities. • **Risk** What is Risk and Risk Management; Risk Management in Projects; Risk Management Strategy; Risk Management Procedure; Risk Budget; Risk Responsibilities. • **Practical Work** Specially written scenarios and comprehensive sets of related tasks help provide a practical application of the method. Practical work includes creating process models, completing tasks related to specific elements of the method such as how the PRINCE2 themes help to apply the PRINCE2 principles as well as a variety of objective test questions. Many tasks are designed to help delegates 'link' the four integrated elements of PRINCE2®; "principles",

Entry Requirements

There are no formal entry requirements for this course. All course content and the examinations are based on the TSO publication "Managing Successful Projects with PRINCE2®" which each delegate will receive as part of their pre-course work pack. We recommend that approximately 10 hours is spent of the pre-course work. A general appreciation of the project environment may prove advantageous to some delegates. Please contact us if you are uncertain about the suitability of this course for your requirements

PRINCE2® is a Registered Trade Mark and a Registered Community Trade Mark of the Office of Government Commerce in the UK and other countries, and is registered in the U.S. Patent and Trademark Office. The Swirl logo™ is a Trade Mark of the Office of Government Commerce. M_o_R®, ITIL® and P3O® are Registered Trade Marks of the Office of Government Commerce. MSP™ is a Trade Mark of the Office of Government Commerce. CAPM®, PMBOK®, PMI® and PMP® are Registered Trade Marks of Project Management Institute, Inc. IPMA® is Registered Trade Mark of International Project Management Association. © 2009-2010 POTIFOB, all rights reserved.

PRINCE2 MASTER CLASS

The prince2 master class is a new concept in senior project management, leadership supervision and oversight. The aim of this course is not to pass the prince2 examination standards but to give first hand tailored knowledge in project management. This is targeted towards top managers of government, government ministries, institutions, and parasatals, corporate organisations, politicians of all calibre, governors, senators, chairpersons, lawmakers, local govt chief executives, and top civil servants.

This is a one week training workshop designed to give these echelons of development a more practical approach to project management. The workshop training is structurally tailored to provide advanced knowledge to leaders of organisations on successful project management oversight. With Nigeria topping the list of countries with the highest number of abandoned projects, this course becomes highly desirable. This training is targeted primarily towards the top managers of govt and private corporate organisations with the hope that it will nevertheless cure the disease of project abandonment and incompletion.

Course Content

This course aims to provide the delegate with a practical knowledge in real life and real time experience of PRINCE2® and covers the theory and practical implementation of the method, in order to deliver the best in real time experience project management and supervision. The syllabus contains the following knowledge areas:

Course Content

- **Tailored Approach to Managing Projects** Setting the scene for a tailored approach to managing all projects; project success criteria; a tailored model of the PRINCE2 method including the integrated elements of principles, processes, themes and tailoring.

- **The Process-based Approach** PRINCE2 focuses on key processes needed for successful project management which must be present, but may be 'tailored' to reflect the complexity, scope and risks faced by the project. SPOCE's PRINCE2 Process Model will be used to help delegates understand and appreciate what should be done to manage each project, why it should be done and when in the project lifecycle.

- **Business Case** What is a Business Case; Outcomes, Outputs, Benefits and Dis-benefits; Developing, Verifying and Maintaining the Business Case; Contents of the Business Case; Confirming the benefits and the Benefits Review Plan; Business Case Responsibilities.

- **Organisation** Project Management Team Structure and the Project Board, Project Assurance, Project Manager, Team Manager, Change Authority and Project Support roles & responsibilities. Stakeholder management; Communication Management Strategy; Organization Responsibilities.

- **Plans** Levels and content of Plans; Exception Plans; Product-based approach to planning – Project Product Description, Product Breakdown Structure, Product Description, Product Flow Diagram; the PRINCE2 planning steps; Plans Responsibilities.

- **Progress** Management and Technical Stages. Tolerance and Raising Exceptions. Project Board and Project Manager Controls for Reviewing and Reporting Progress; Baselines for Control; Capturing and Reporting Lessons; Event-driven and time-driven controls; Progress Responsibilities.

- **Change** Issue and Change Control procedure; Configuration Management procedure; Configuration Management Strategy; Baselining, handling changes to, tracking and protecting products. Change Authority and Change Budget; Change Responsibilities.

- **Quality** Quality Defined, The Quality Audit Trial; Quality; Acceptance Criteria, Quality Criteria, Quality Management Strategy, Quality Assurance, Quality Controls and Quality Review technique; Quality Responsibilities.

- **Risk** What is Risk and Risk Management; Risk Management in Projects; Risk Management Strategy; Risk Management Procedure; Risk Budget; Risk Responsibilities.

- **Practical Work** Specially written scenarios and comprehensive sets of related tasks help provide a practical application of the method. Practical work includes creating process models, completing tasks related to specific elements of the method such as how the PRINCE2 themes help to apply the PRINCE2 principles as well as a variety of objective test questions. Many tasks are designed to help delegates 'link' the four integrated elements of PRINCE2®; "principles",

Benefits of using PRINCE2

Organisations are becoming increasingly aware of the opportunities for adopting a project approach to the way that they address business change. They are aware of the benefits that a single, common, structured method for project management can bring:
- A method that is repeatable
- A method that is teachable
- Building on experience
- Ensuring that everyone knows what to expect, where, how and when
- Early warning of problems
- Being proactive, not reactive, but able to accommodate sudden, unexpected events.

Projects may exist in their own right, may have relationships with other projects or may be part of a larger programme of work. PRINCE2 is applicable in all these situations. PRINCE2 provides the organisation with:
- Controlled management of change, in terms of investment and return on investment
- Active involvement of users and stakeholders throughout the project to ensure that the product(s) will meet the business, functional, environmental, service and management requirements
- An approach which distinguishes the management of the project from the development of the product(s), so that the management approach is the same whether the project is to build a ship or implement new working practices.

PRINCE2 provides benefits to the managers and directors of a project and to an organisation, through the controllable use of resources and the ability to manage risk more effectively.

PRINCE2 embodies established and proven best practice in project management. It is widely recognised and understood, providing a common language for all participants in a project.

PRINCE2 encourages formal recognition of responsibilities within a project and focuses on what a project is to deliver, why, when and for whom.

PRINCE2 provides projects with:
- A controlled and organised start, middle and end
- Regular reviews of progress against plan and against the Business Case
- Flexible decision points
- Automatic management control of any deviations from the plan
- The involvement of management and stakeholders at the right time during the project
- Good communication channels between the project management team and the rest of the organisation
- Agreement on the required quality at the outset and continuous monitoring against those requirements.

Project Managers using PRINCE2 are able to:
- Establish terms of reference as a prerequisite to the start of a project
- Use a defined structure for delegation, authority and communication
- Divide the project into manageable stages for more accurate planning
- Ensure that resource commitment from management is part of any approval to proceed
- Provide regular, but brief, management reports
- Keep meetings with management and stakeholders to a minimum but at the vital points in the project.

Those who will be directly involved with using the products or outcomes of a project are able to:
- Participate in all the decision making on a project
- If desired, be fully involved in day-to-day progress
- Participate in quality checks throughout the project
- Ensure that their requirements are being adequately satisfied.

For senior management of the project, PRINCE2 uses the 'management by exception' concept, i.e. management agree a plan, and then let the Project Manager get on with it unless

something is forecast to go wrong. Senior managers are kept fully informed of the project status without having to attend frequent, time-consuming meetings.

PRINCE2®
PRINCE2® is a Registered Trade Mark and a Registered Community Trade Mark of the Office of Government Commerce in the UK and other countries, and is registered in the U.S. Patent and Trademark Office. The Swirl logo™ is a Trade Mark of the Office of Government Commerce. M_o_R®, ITIL® and P3O® are Registered Trade Marks of the Office of Government Commerce. MSP™ is a Trade Mark of the Office of Government Commerce. CAPM®, PMBOK®, PMI® and PMP® are Registered Trade Marks of Project Management Institute, Inc. IPMA® is Registered Trade Mark of International Project Management Association. © 2009-2010 POTIFOB, all rights reserved.

2. MOBILE CYBER INSTITUTE (MCI)

INTRODUCTION

After a year study, we became genuinely alarmed at the rate and extent of computer illiteracy and cyber-phobia among Nigerian masses. As a result, Heathrow Cyber Services Nig Ltd wants to bridge this gap by offering to provide computer literacy, web training and ICT skills throughout the country. This will be offered in the form of a Mobile Institute. Just like the name implies it is completely a mobile school. This is packaged as a 2 week intensive class room training at any premises: you don't have to go to school anymore, school comes to you. We are determined bring the training to you and best of all it is affordable. For only N7, 000 naira per candidate we teach candidates to become computer and internet literate in 2 weeks. We come with our own computers and equipment so you don't have to bring yours. We teach step by step, face to face and practically. We begin from the known to the unknown and in a matter of 2 weeks candidates will earn a prestigious INTERNATIONAL ICT certificate from us. The certification is endorsed by the Nigerian government through NETPOST. This is the fastest way to become computer and web literate guaranteed. Our key target is to get majority of Nigerians computer and web literate by making training available, accessible and affordable. Our vision is to get more than 80% of the Nigerian masses computer and web literate by 2020.

A SAMPLE OF OUR TRACT RECORD SO FAR

MCI LAGOS TRAINING SESSION July 2011

MCI LAGOS GRADUATION 31ST JULY 2011

MCI KANO
ABUJA

MCI

Detail syllabus and Course Contents

Module 1	Content	Topic

Computer Application	Module aim and objectives	
	Component of a PC	• Keyboard • Mouse • CPU • Monitor • Printers • Scanners • Backup Systems (Tape drives, jazz drives, Zip drives, etc.) • Modems • And other Peripherals
	Making PCs work for you	**Using Applications-** • Word • Outlook Express • PowerPoint • Excel • Access • etc.
	Changing Nature of Computer	• Tablet PCs • Palm Tops • Speech Recognition • Flash drive • Flat screens • Computer Cell Phone Interface • Wireless Computing – hotspot • Digital Cameras • USB ports • etc.
Module 2	**Content**	**Topic**
Internet Usage and Awareness	**Module aim and objectives**	
	Internet basic	• What is the Internet • Why use the Internet • Main street cyberspace • How it all began
	The World Wide Web	• How the web works • Web Pages and Websites • Home sweet home page • Hyperlinks • Domain names • Web Addresses • Anatomy of the Web • Web browsers • Launching your browser • Navigating the web • Browser anatomy • The Toolbar • The Location Box • The Menu Bar • The Access Indicator • The Status Bar • The Scroll Bar • Some Browser Tricks • Bookmarks • Tips for Faster Surfing

Communicating & Collaborating	Module aim and objectives	
	Introducing e-mail	• Using e-mail • Delivering e-mail • E-mail privacy and encryption • The e-mail message header
	Using e-mail	• Configuring your e-mail software • Using Outlook Express • Sending and receiving messages • Understanding E-mail • Anatomy of an E-mail message • Step-by-step: sending an E-mail • Reading E-mail messages • Attaching Files • Step-by-step Sending E-mail Attachments • Opening Attachments • Managing your E-mail messages • Smileys • Abbreviations • Finding E-mail Addresses • E-mail Etiquette
	Internet chat	• Real-time conversation • Using Microsoft Chat
	Video conferencing	• Virtual meetings • Using Netmeeting
	Finding Information Online	• Searching For Information • Google, Yahoo, MSN
	What to do Online INTERNET SOCIAL NETWORKING	• Play Games • Send mail • Online Study . facebook, skype, youtube etc
	Exercise	• Sending e-mail • Searching for materials on the web • Downloading and storing web based Information on your Computer.

3. ICT TECHNICAL COURSES: INSTRUCTOR LED TRAINING
SPECIAL COURSES ON OFFER IN THIS PROPOSAL

MOS Certification Training Course: Microsoft Office Specialist - Office 2010 Training Course

The Microsoft Office Specialist (MOS) Training Package from Heathrow Cyber Services include expert instructor-led training modules with customized presentations, practice exam simulators and learning supplements for an all-inclusive training program that provides all the benefits of classroom training at your own pace.

Heathrow Cyber Services's MOS 2010 Training Package includes the following exams:

- Microsoft Word 2010
- Microsoft Excel 2010
- Microsoft Access 2010
- Microsoft PowerPoint 2010
- Microsoft Outlook 2010

The Microsoft Office Specialist (MOS) credential, part of the Microsoft Business Certification program, identifies specific skills covering the most in-demand 2010 Microsoft Office system products—Microsoft Office Word 2010, Excel 2010, PowerPoint 2010, Access 2010, and Outlook 2010. The MCAS certification is replacing the Microsoft Office Specialist or MOS certification.

Heathrow Cyber Services's Office 2010 MOS Certification training courses prepare students for the MOS exams by teaching greater skill mastery in each of the individual Microsoft Office 2010 programs. Candidates must pass one or more certification exams in order to earn the MOS credential. The MOS exams provide a valid and reliable measure of technical proficiency and expertise in Microsoft Office 2010 by evaluating the ability to use the advanced features in the products to solve real-world business problems.

You can be certain that **Heathrow Cyber Services's** comprehensive **MOS training course** will provide you with all the tools necessary to successfully prepare for your **MOS certification.**

ECDL Certification Training Course- European Computer Drivers License
The **European Computer Driving License (ECDL)** is the world's largest end-user computer skills certification program, with over seven million candidates in 146 Countries. The **ECDL** is a vendor-neutral certification for users that need to demonstrate to an international standard that they are fully-competent in the use of a personal computer and common computer applications and that they know the essential concepts of Information Technology. **ECDL Core V 4.0** has been approved for the following software applications: Open Office, Star Office, XP, 2003, MAC and Lotus Smartsuite.

HCS's **ECDL certification training course** will teach students essential IT knowledge/skills, core IT skills applicable in any software environment, and increased confidence in computer use while giving the student a platform of basic knowledge from which to move on to higher-level IT education. **HCS** is so certain our **ECDL training course** meets and exceeds the exam objectives.

CompTIA A+ 2009 Certification Training Courses

220-701 Essentials & 220-702 Practical Application

Heathrow Cyber Services offers you the most effective way to earn your CompTIA A+ 2009 certification. Heathrow Cyber Services's CompTIA A+ 2009 Essentials & Practical Application teaches students the competence in areas such as installation, preventative maintenance, networking, security, troubleshooting, customer service and communication skills to work with clients.

After completing this course, students will know hardware, laptops, motherboards, processors, memory, CPU, troubleshooting theory, preventative maintenance techniques, Windows XP, Windows Vista, cables, connectors, network types, SOHO network, security concepts, security technologies, viruses, malware, communication and professionalism.

CompTIA A+ Essentials measures the necessary competencies of an entry-level IT professional with a recommended 500 hours of hands-on experience in the lab or field. It tests for the fundamentals of computer technology, networking and security, as well as the communication skills and professionalism now required of all entry-level IT professionals.

CompTIA A+ Practical Application is an extension of the knowledge and skills identified in CompTIA A+ Essentials, with more of a "hands-on" orientation focused on scenarios in which troubleshooting and tools must be applied to resolve problems.

Heathrow Cyber Services's course curriculum is either CAQC (CompTIA Authorized Quality Curriculum) or in the process of becoming CAQC, ensuring you receive the training and knowledge needed to succeed.

MCITP Server Administrator Certification Training Courses: Microsoft Certified IT Professional

The Microsoft **MCITP Server Administrator Training Courses** from **Heathrow Cyber Services** include expert instructor-led training modules with customized presentations, practice exam simulators and learning supplements for an all-inclusive training program that provides all the benefits of classroom training at your own pace.

Earning the **MCITP: Server Administrator certification** distinguishes you as an IT professional committed to excellence in working with Windows Server 2008. **Microsoft Server administrators** are recognized among their peers and managers as leaders in the daily operations management of Windows Server 2008.

Heathrow Cyber Services's MCITP Server Administrator training courses teaches students the knowledge and skills needed to implement, monitor, and maintain Windows Server 2008 servers, to configure identity and access solutions with Windows Server 2008 Active Directory and to implement networking features and functionalities in Windows Server 2008. Microsoft's Professional Series credentials validate a comprehensive set of skills required to be successful on the job. These skills include project management, operations management, and planning, and they are contextual to the job role. By

validating a comprehensive set of skills, these credentials give candidates and their hiring managers a reliable indicator of on-the-job performance.
You can be certain that **Heathrow Cyber Services's** comprehensive **MCITP training courses** will provide you with all the tools necessary to successfully prepare for your **MCITP certifications.**

4. Laptop Easy Acquisition Program: LEAP

A LAPTOP ACQUISITION OFFER
BY
HEATHROW CYBER SERVICES NIG LTD

INTRODUCTION

The Laptop Easy Acquisition Program (LEAP), is designed to leap Nigerian masses up technologically by helping them acquire a laptop pc with ease. The business world and the market place are now dominated by information and communication technology (ICT). Owning a pc is no longer a luxury but a necessity. An average Nigerian now needs to communicate online and to keep pace with all the many channels of communication online, one requires a modern technology enabled personal computer (PC). Many Nigerians therefore desire as a matter of necessity to own a pc but cannot afford one. To purchase a pc that is cable of keeping pace with technology costs between NGN85,000 – NGN250,000 naira. Few employees can afford to cough out such large amount from their meagre salaries without great inconvenience. LEAP is therefore designed to provide an affordable solution making it easy for the masses to acquire a laptop pc with ease as the cost is spread over time from 6 months to 12 months. Working with Banks who have signed up to the program, loan facilities can be secured to finance the LEAP program.

Under the scheme, Heathrow Cyber Services Nig Ltd is able to source the acquisition of laptops with top manufacturers in Europe and the US and deliver to interested parties. Through this method and with bank grantee for the scheme, the bank pays for the purchase while beneficiaries pay for the machines over time with deductions made on a monthly basis. For example a pc of NGN110,000 naira will only cost NGN 9,200 Naira a month over 12 months, making it affordable to the employee on flexible payment terms. Moreover, with low interest charges from the banks there can never be a better time to acquire a pc. To apply please call the numbers at the end of the last page and our representative will speak with you immediately. Equipment specifications are available on request.

5. EMPLOYMENT TRAINING WORKSHOP

INTRODUCTION

The Employability Academy (TEA) is of the view that a high percentage of Job seekers in Nigeria are unable to find employment simply because they are unemployable. Candidates lack the skills employers are looking for. Increasingly, organisations are seeking flexible employees who can adapt to change, are effective in operating in interdisciplinary environment, have confidence in public engagement, presentation, customer care, superior product knowledge, have developed interpersonal skills and have ICT skills. Our workshop aims to develop these skills in candidates over the six weeks training period. There is great skills gap that exists in Nigeria today. The gap is between skilled and non-skilled workers. This has created a huge unemployment among Nigerian youths that is now endemic. Many graduate youths in Nigeria cannot put bread and **TEA** on the table. Nigeria today has one of the highest numbers of unskilled workforce in the job market. A two year survey carried out revealed this fact. These graduate youths simply do not have the necessary skills that employers require in a complex business world dominated by ICT. The Nigerian educational system is flawed in design to emphasize the acquisition of head knowledge rather than practical (SKILL) application of knowledge. I have met a computer science graduate from Nigeria who has never touched a PC. Needless, to say this is the lot of many graduate youths scattered across the country looking for jobs endlessly. The unemployment crises in Nigeria have reached a climax that if left unchecked could resort into social unrest. It is to this end that we want to make a difference. We want to borrow a leave from the EU and promote systematic skills acquisition in Nigeria. One undeniable evidence of European greatness is their investment in the education of their people, because the Europeans know that education is the bedrock of economic development. So even after formal education European Governments continue to invest in developing the skills of their people including those who are already in full time employment. Our company runs a govt funded grant programme in the UK to train managers and directors of small businesses to equip them with new skills. The govt invests billions of pounds into this programme annually. It is because the govt knows that small businesses are the driving force of economic growth. The bulk of unemployed graduate youths need to be retrained and equipped with new and modern skills especially in ICT. The purpose of this proposal is to define ways that can be used to tackle unemployment in Nigeria. That's why we have as our motto and slogan, "Training for Jobs"! Yes, that's exactly what our training certifications will offer Nigerian youths, employability!

SKILLS GAP TRAINING WORKSHOP

Our Employment Training Workshop is aimed at addressing these shortcomings. We hope to bridge identified skills gap and competencies required in order to improve a candidate's eligibility when seeking employment. The Workshop aims to develop business management and personal skills. In consultation with employers, the workshop focuses on those skills which are recognised as important for personal development in preparation for a future career in a professional or management role working in the public, private or voluntary sector.

BENEFITS & LEARNING OUTCOME

Retention and Employment opportunities for best performing candidates with work placement organisations. Improved competitiveness in job search as a result of newly acquired skills and work experience. Awareness of the skills and personal qualities that employers most value in graduate employees.

Aims to develop the breadth of your business knowledge and to provide you with the key skills demanded by employers. Aims to develop knowledge and skills in key areas of management, decision-making, leadership, negotiation and entrepreneurship. Able to critically assess how an individual matches up to employers requirements.

Begin to consider ways in which they as individuals might acquire more of these key skills and personal qualities.

Learn about personal development planning as one way of structuring their reflection on their new knowledge and skills.

STRUCTURE

The workshop is a mix of classroom sessions and work placement opportunities. The work placement is a unique feature of the workshop as it compliments what the candidates are taught in the classroom with real life business experience.

WORKSHOP CONTENT

The workshop covers the following topics

- Team Working
- Leadership
- Business Ethics
- Communication
- Entrepreneurship
- Research Methodology
- Numeracy
- Decision Making
- Use of Information Technology
- Negotiation Skills
- Inter-personal skills

TARGET AUDIENCE

Fresh and Recent Graduates

Long Term Unemployed

Career Changers

6. THE NIGERIAN POLITICIAN TRAINNG COURSE

INTRODUCTION

The 'Nigerian Politician' training workshop programme is designed to give the elected representative of the people complete overview of his public and civic responsibility. The electorate have certain expectations of their political leaders and those who represent their interest in the political structure. This course is design to help Nigerian politicians understand what these expectations are and to provide a complete synopsis training exposure that meets these expectations.

After undertaking this programme you will be better positioned to face the challenges associated with political responsibility and accountability. This programme will make the Nigerian politician not only to be accountable to the people but also become more knowledgeable about his role and what the public expects from him. The programme is not designed to expose political failure but create enabling platform for political success. Political career can be greatly rewarding and a path to fulfilling dreams and aspirations when political ethics are correctly applied and adhered to.

It is my understanding that this programme will set the pedestal for neo-political emancipation and reprogramming of the thinking process of Nigerian political leaders to fulfil their roles as great statesmen and women.

The training workshop will be led and delivered by Dr Joshua Jogo, one of Britain's great political thinkers and political coach of our time. He will lead a team of prominent British politicians, including members of the Cabinet and Parliament in interactive and participatory political brainstorming sessions.
Dr Jogo is excited to visit Nigeria and take a political team of Nigerian Political Leaders to Britain as part of this exciting and mind blowing political adventure. This is a ten day training program to be held in the United Kingdom at our prestigious centre for leadership and management.

Please find below a complete course outline for this training programme.

Programme 1:

Day1 is for travel to the UK: approximately six hours of flight and enough time to rest in preparation for the next day's business.

Day 2 is a research day that enables delegates to truly discover what the general public think of politicians. This should however, only begin after they have designed a questionnaire during the first 1½ hour session that each person will then use as their template. Furthermore, Day 4 is used to analyse research findings, undertake further research if required and/or use the information gained for inclusion on Day 5.

Programme 2:

5 days programme to be held in London (including a two day tour of political institutions and houses of parliament) Delegates will also have the opportunity to meet some top political leaders in Britain including members of British Parliament.

It is recommended that day numbered 2 and 4 are "tour days" to allow many open conversations to be undertaken – some of which might then be used during the following workshop discussions!

Timings; Please note these are suggested timings and may be altered according to circumstances and during each day as the programme progresses. The timing /tour plans are designed around requirements as part of the training programme.
Day 2; Westminster Abbey and Houses of Parliament.
Day 4; Buckingham Palace and Canterbury Cathedral.

Main Issues / Programme Topics To Be Covered:

PART A:
- Honesty / Integrity / Credibility
- Ethics / Ethical Behaviour
- Fraud / Fraudulent Behaviour
- Professional Political Behaviour

PART B:
- What do you want to achieve as a politician?
- What is your future design for your career?
- Who is your customer? (the voter) and what do they want from you as their politician?
- Setting standards of behaviour
- What are the standards by which all politicians should abide by?

a) As a voter, what standards of behaviour do you expect from your politician?
b) What standards of behaviour should the electorate expect from us?

Is there a difference between a) and b)?

Draft Proposal and Programme Time Table

Day 1: The Role of the Politician

Session Subjects/Topics

Session 1
(9.15 – 10.45)
- Welcome and Domestics
- Introduction
- Knowing You – Knowing Me
- Planning your future career
- Why are we here and what do we want to achieve?
- Programme Overview

Morning Break
(10.45 – 11.00)

Session 2
(11.00 – 12.30)
UNDERSTANDING YOUR CUSTOMER – THE VOTER
- Who and where is your customer/voter?
- What do we think they are seeking from their politician?
- What expectations do they have of politicians?

Lunch
(12.30 – 13.15)

Session 3
(13.15 – 14.45)
UNDERSTANDING YOUR CUSTOMER – THE VOTER - Continued
- Do We Understand the political opinions of the local community?
- How do we meet their expectations?
- Other voter issues for consideration?

Afternoon Break
(14.45 – 15.00)

Session 4

(15.00 – 16.30)
THE POLITICIAN – What or who is a politician?
- The role of the modern politician – What is it?
- Is a good politician born or are they made/trained?
- Other people's perceptions of politicians – Do we **really know** what these are?

Day 3: Effectiveness/ Efficiency / Needs of the community

Session Subjects/Topics

Session 1
(9.15 – 10.45)
RECOGNISING THE TRULY EFFECTIVE POLITICIAN
- Good and poor political performance - How does this appear to us?
- What are the Key Qualities and Skills of a Modern Politician?

Morning Break
(10.45 – 11.00)

Session 2
(11.00 – 12.30)
COMMUNICATIONS AND THE TRULY EFFECTIVE POLITICIAN
- How important is Communication **And** logical thinking?
- How do we ensure we do not say the wrong thing at the wrong time?

Lunch
(12.30 – 13.15)

Session 3
(13.15 – 14.45)
THE POLITICIAN AS A LEADER
- Begin the key political skills Improvement process;
  - Communications
  - Leadership.
- Is communications and leadership the same thing?

Afternoon Break
(14.45 – 15.00)

Session 4
(15.00 – 16.30)
DECISION MAKING AND TAKING
- Define the decision making issue & who is or might be affected by it
- Understanding & complying with Fiduciary Duty
- Maintaining integrity / avoiding fraud and fraudulent behaviour
  - Cognitive Dissonance
  - The Stakeholder effect!
- Justifying decisions (or, it seemed like a good idea at the time!!)

Day 5: Personal/ Political Behaviour & Ethics

Session Subjects/Topics

Session 1
(9.15 – 10.45)
ETHICAL CONDUCT
- Do we know and recognise what Ethical Conduct is and what it looks like to

people generally?
- How important is this issue to you in an increasingly global economy?
- How much effect does this issue have on our appearance as politicians?
- Establishing ethical conduct standards for modern politicians in a modern society.

Morning Break
(10.45 – 11.00)

Session 2
(11.00 – 12.30)
STANDARDS AND INTEGRITY
- What standards are required?
- What are those standards required to achieve and with whom?
- How important is integrity and how much should we protect "our" integrity?
- How much should and are we concerned with Human Rights?
- What effect might any lack of concern we display concerning Human Rights have on our political career?

Lunch
(12.30 – 13.15)

Session 3
(13.15 – 14.45)
WHAT HAVE WE ACHIEVED SO FAR?
- Assessing progress – Have we progressed during this event and if so how much?
- What has been achieved and by whom?
- What will each of us do differently as a result of this programme and our time together?
- Action Planning – individual /collective action plans to be designed

Afternoon Break
(14.45 – 15.00)

Session 4
(15.00 – 16.30)
THE FUTURE
- Using the Action Plans – each delegate will give a short (10 minute) presentation that commits them to an improved political future and career

Conference and Programme Speakers

RON STRADLING

ABOUT RON STRADLING

Ron is UK's most versatile political and ethical coach. After twenty successful years in sales and service during which he gained wholesaling experience, and then in senior general management roles in vehicle retailing, Ron subsequently sought to utilise his extensive knowledge and experience to help politicians and business executives become more efficient and effective. Since 1989 he has assisted many different political affiliations by providing expertise in numerous areas, including strategic planning, govt planning, business performance management, senior management development and leadership skills, change management programmes, effective communications and customer care. Not surprisingly, Ron is passionate about helping both individuals achieve their full potential. He is a SFEDI qualified political and business mentor, a verified Motor Industry Consultant, a Fellow of the Institute of Business Consulting (FIBC), and received the Institute of Business Adviser's Growth Adviser of the Year 2006 Award. Ron has helped organisations, irrespective of their size, overcome their specific challenges. His flexible approach enables you to receive training, mentoring, coaching, advice and / or a combination of these as may be appropriate to your individual circumstances and requirements. His wide experience gained in the "real world" by people who have been there, done it and are still doing it has been effectively used in organisations of all sizes including start-ups and multi-nationals, government departments and even island communities.

ORGANISER AND CONVENER: THE NIGERIAN POLITICAN CONFRENCE:

About Joshua Jogo

DR JOSHUA JOGO

Joshua Jogo is a Nigerian Born British Politician with love for political innovation and strategy in a changing society. His political slogan is 'integrity and accountability are twin brothers'. He is the community spokesman of the Conservative Party for Stanwell and Stanwell Moor based in Staines, Middlesex, United Kingdom. He is a member of the Spelthorne Conservative Association and serves as a member on the committee board representing his local constituency of Stanwell and Stanwell Moor, a predominately English constituency. He was the first black ever to win nomination to run for office on the platform of the Conservative Party in Surrey. In 2008 he ran for County Council Elections in Surrey where he nearly unseated the incumbent. He lost the elections by few votes. He made history due to his community activism and today due to his political prowess there is an elected black member of parliament for Spelthorne. Mr Kwasi Kwateng MP, a Black British of Ghanaian parentage got elected as the first Black MP for Spelthorne.

Joshua is passionate about seen political change occur in Nigeria where the rule of law, social justice, integrity, honesty, transparency and accountability are the hallmarks of the Nigerian political process.

He is an educator and the CEO of Heathrow Training Services Ltd UK and Heathrow Cyber Services Nig Ltd.

He runs a centre for Leadership and Management Science based at Heathrow Airport, United Kingdom and oversees a skills acquisition programme funded by the British Government in the UK. Due to his unflinching passion for youth development and Skills acquisition he established Heathrow Cyber Services Nig Ltd, an ICT training company to promote ICT and project management skills acquisition in Nigeria. In October 2010, Heathrow Cyber Services Nig Ltd signed a Strategy Partnership Agreement with NETPOST NIGERIA LTD, an associate company of NIPOST to offer ICT training throughout the country using the platform provided by the post offices.

Joshua Jogo is an ordained Minister of the Gospel and he is married with three children.

Conference and programme Speaker

About Matthew A. Daniel.

Matthew A. Daniel

Matthew is a British based leadership and change expert. A management consultant of over twenty year's experience, he has worked in various roles in the fashion, literary, furniture, pharmaceuticals, I.T and educational sectors. He worked in the British Pharmaceutical industry in business development across the top 3 pharmaceutical companies winning many awards for achievement the most notable being territorial business manager of the year in 2002 in the Boehringer/Pfizer project in which an award was given in Prague (Czech republic).He left Johnson and Johnson in 2005 to concentrate on consultancy to various firms in the UK.

Matthew has been educated in some of the best schools in the world with his pursuit taking him through University of Ibadan, Cambridge, Oxford and Oxford Brookes. He is an associate of British Pharmaceutical Industry (A.B.P.I), A certified project manager (Prince 2), a Neuro- Linguistic Programmer(N.L.P) a Cisco certified network associate (CCNA), a trained teacher (PGCE) and a member of the chartered institute of marketing (CIM).

Matthew is currently involved as a Senior Consultant to Heathrow Training Services (UK) and a Director of Heathrow Cyber Services Nig Ltd. He has an unflinching believe that it's our time in Africa and Nigeria has a pivotal role to play in that transformation. Matthew is married with three children.

ADDITIONAL RECOMMENDED TRAINING FOR NIGERIAN POLITICIANS

PRINCE2 MASTER CLASS

The prince2 master class is a new concept in senior project management, leadership supervision and oversight. The aim of this course is not to pass the prince2 examination standards but to give first hand tailored knowledge in project management. This is targeted towards top managers of government, government ministries, institutions, and parasatals, corporate organisations, politicians of all calibre, governors, senators, chairpersons, lawmakers, local govt chief executives, and top civil servants.

This is a five day training workshop designed to give the echelons of development a more practical approach to project management. The workshop training is structurally tailored to provide advanced knowledge to leaders of organisations on successful project management oversight. With Nigeria topping the list of countries with the highest number of abandoned projects, this course becomes highly desirable. This training targeted primarily towards top managers of govt and private projects will nevertheless cure the disease of project abandonment and incompletion.

COMPREHENSIVE LIST OF ICT COURSES THAT WE OFFER ON

Project Management and Best Practice - *New*
PRINCE2 Foundation
PRINCE2 Practitioner
APM Introductory
Managing Risk in Projects
MSP 2007 Foundation
Programme and Project Sponsorship
ITIL v3 Foundation
ISO/IEC20000

Microsoft Certification
MCITP
  Database Administrator
  Database Administrator 2008
  Database Developer
  Database Developer 2008
  Enterprise Administrator
  Server Administrator
  Enterprise Messaging Admin
  Enterprise Support
  Consumer Support
MCTS
MCDST
MCSA
  MCSA 2003
  MCSA Messaging

Oracle 10g OCA
Oracle 11g OCA
Crystal Reports XI
IT Training Library
iPod with Training Library
VMWare vSphere 4.0

CompTIA Certification
CompTIA A+
CompTIA Network +
CompTIA Security +
CompTIA Project +
CompTIA CDIA +
CompTIA Server +
CompTIA Linux+
CompTIA PDI +
CompTIA Training Library

Cisco Certification
Cisco CCENT
Cisco CCNA
Cisco CCNA Security
Cisco CCNP

  MCSA Security
MCSE
  MCSE 2003
  MCSE Messaging
  MCSE Security
MCPD
MCP
MOS: Office 2000, XP & 2003 Professional
MCAS: Office 2007
MCAS: Office 2010

EC-Council
CEH
CNDA
CHFI
ECSA/LPT
MSS Masters of Security Science
Security5

Others
CISSP
CISA
CWNA
ECDL
ITIL v3 Foundation
ICDL

Our IT Course Bundles Include* :

- Expert Instructor led training delivered via video streaming
- 24hr expert help and student support for 1 year / 2 years (dependant on bundle)
- Extensive Demonstrations and presentations delivered in a multimedia format
- Practice Tests
- Simulation Exams
- Online access for 1 year/ 2 years dependant on bundle
- Significant Savings!!

* Most of our courses include Practice Tests and some include Simulated Lab learning. **Flexibility**

HEATHROW TRAINING SERVICES LTD UK
COMPANY PROFILE

Heathrow Training Services Ltd is a UK based cutting edge training and educational resources company established in the 21st century to pioneer and catalyze a modern concept in education and training export. Over the years we have established a recognised and respected brand in the training industry. Since inception in 2006 then known as Heathrow Specialist Training Services the company has grown from strength to strength becoming one of the leading providers of Leadership, Management and professional IT certification training in the UK.

During this time we have developed a new strategy and approach to services for our numerous clients. We have realised the need to work with other suppliers and partners in all areas. We have built up a network of 'partner' companies that now means that we can offer you a vast range of services. In addition to our renowned provision of E learning and on-site

IT training including our fast selling Prince2 Management Training Courses. We can offer public scheduled courses in all areas with discounts. We can also source training solutions in just about any sector that you can imagine. We can help procure the best value software and hardware and provide you with consultants to set-up and support. Do you need to recruit IT staff? We can help at a much lower rate than offered by 'traditional' recruitment agencies. In addition we can provide consultants in database management, website design and marketing specialists. If you have a project that needs to be delivered on-time and within budget we have the knowledge to get you the most suitable professionals for the role at the best rate! HTS is therefore one point of contact for everything you need in the industry.

STRATEGIC PARTNERSHIP WITH THE GOVERNMENT OF GREAT BRITAIN

In recognition of the company's numerous contributions in the recruitment and delivery of government funded training for skills development and acquisition, working on various training schemes including the former Train To Gain programme under the defunct Learning and Skills Council, HTS is an approved major provider of Leadership and Management Training under the govt's Leadership and Management Funded Programme now delivered though the Skills Funding Agency. HTS considers this as a strategic and unique partnership with the govt to train, up skill, empower, and equip businesses with leadership and management skills during and after the financial downturn. Under the scheme HTS in partnership with Skills Funding Agency (SFA) as an approved direct provider is able to train leaders of all businesses that employ between 5 – 249 staff. Up to £1000 pounds of govt funded grant is available under the programme to meet the training needs of businesses that are eligible under the scheme. This is a contract worth £36 million pounds to deliver leadership and management training to 4000 businesses each across nine regions of Great Britain per year. Below are the regions and partners covered by HTS in its delivery of the Leadership and Management Grant Training Programme.

Region	Organization	Telephone Number
London	Exemplas	01707 398204
South East	SEEDA	01483 484200
East Of England	TCHC	01923 698450
East Midlands	East Midlands Business Ltd	01332 826400
South West	Northern Arc Ltd	01275 370861
West Midlands	West Midlands Brokerage Services	08000 754 557
North East	Northumberland Business Services	01915 166767
North West	Business Link North West	0845 602 0062
Yorkshire & Humberside	Exemplas	01707 398204

Between 2010 and 2011 alone, HTS has trained over 700 companies and charities under the programme and counting.

Our Training Locations in the UK

Canary Wharf Training Centre

Our flagship training centre at Canary Wharf enjoys stunning panoramic views of London from the 33rd floor in the heart of docklands, overlooking the O2 dome and the River Thames. 25 Canada Square is one of the tallest buildings in docklands and is shared with Citigroup. It's a great place to learn.

The training centre is very close to the Jubilee Line at Canary Wharf tube station.

+ Address details & more information

Level 33 25 Canada Square Canary Wharf
London
E14 5LQ

London (City) Training Centre

Our training centre in Monument is set on the 1st floor of Providian House - an imposing city building that stands commandingly on Monument Street. Only minutes from Monument Station, and a short walk to Cannon Street, this centre is beautifully connected allowing easy access.

+ Address details & more information

Providian House Monument Street London
EC3R 8AJ

Reading Training Centre

The HTS training centre in Reading provides a first class learning environment and is conveniently located less than quarter of a mile from junction 11 of the M4 and only 10 minutes from Reading town centre.

+ Address details & more information

Atlantic House Imperial Way Reading
RG2 0TD

Bracknell Training Centre

Excellent training facilities in arguably the most prominent building in Bracknell. This training centre is close to the town's many shops and local amenities and is a 5 minute walk from the train station. Bracknell is conveniently located close to both the M3 and M4 motorways.

+ Address details & more information

Atrium Court The Ring Bracknell Berkshire
RG12 1BW

Milton Keynes Training Centre

Our training centre is located in the central business and retail district of Milton Keynes, offering easy access to major roads including the M1 and is a short walk from Milton Keynes train station.

+ Address details & more information

494 Midsummer Boulevard Milton Keynes
MK9 2EA

Manchester Training Centre

The HTS Manchester training centre is located on King Street in the heart of Manchester's central business district, M2 and just a 10 minute walk from Manchester's Piccadilly and Victoria stations. In a vibrant area, the training centre is surrounded by designer outlets, cafes, bars and restaurants.

+ Address details & more information

Pall Mall Court 61 - 67 King Street
Manchester
M2 4PD

Birmingham Training Centre

Our Birmingham training centre is strategically placed within Birmingham's business and retail centre and enjoys excellent transport links.

A recent and extensive regeneration programme has revitalised the centre of Birmingham is a great place to train in the Midlands. The Birmingham training centre is close to a range of new designer stores, cafes, bars and restaurants, and the area is home to a wide range of national and international companies.

+ Address details & more information

43 Temple Row Birmingham
B2 5LS

Bristol Training Centre

HTS's Bristol training centre is located in the tallest building in Bristol. It provides easy access to Bristol's excellent transport networks, in particular an immediate route to the M32 and is only a short walk from Bristol Temple Meads rail station. The training centre also benefits from views of Castle Green Park.

+ Address details & more information

Bristol Castlemead Lower Castle Street
Bristol
BS1 3AG

Edinburgh Training Centre

HTS training facilities in the heart of Edinburgh's beautiful Georgian New Town in St Andrew Square. Overlooking this picturesque city, this is an excellent place to learn. 9-10 St Andrew Square is a listed office building and the Square itself is home to many of Scotland's leading companies and financial institutions. Our Edinburgh training centre is located close to the very best of Scotland's shopping and restaurants, with Jenners dept store, Harvey Nichols and St James Centre all only a few minutes' walk away. Edinburgh train station is also only a 5 minute trip and many bus routes run by this centre.

+ Address detail

9-10 St. Andrew Square Edinburgh Scotland
EH2 2AF

HTS MANAGEMENT TEAM

JOSHUA JOGO
MD/CEO

ELIZABETH NGOZI JOGO
DIRECTOR (FINANCE)

PROF AVONG ZAKKA BONET
ASSOCIATE DIRECTOR

RACHEL EMENIKE
Company Secretary/Solicitor

30 support staff and training consultants

Heathrow Training Services Limited
9 ELIZABETHAN WAY, STANWELL
STAINES, MIDDLESEX
TW19 7QJ
UNITED KINGDOM
Tel: 01784559313
Business Mobile: +447448522120
NIGERIA: +2347063971477
For free Training Needs Analysis (TNA) advice from our Training Consultants:

- Drop us an email to joshuajogo@hotmail.com or
- Visit www.heathrowtrainingservices.com and send an enquiry form.

Heathrow Training Services Limited is a training and educational Centre. We work with over 700 companies and charity organisations across the UK. We also run a centre for management and leadership training. Taking the government's objective to help individuals, businesses and voluntary organisations in the recession and to create more jobs, HTS is a strategic partner in progress. Our vision is to help individuals, businesses and voluntary organisations by promoting part of a government's initiative to train and equip businesses with the necessary skills that they require in order to succeed through and after the recession.

MEMBER

Heathrow Cyber Services Nigeria Ltd
Registered in Nigeria RC 918214
Heathrow Training Services Limited
Registered in England and Wales certificate no. 06965458

MEMBER UK Official Training Provider (UKRLP) Number: 10029365

CONTACT INFORMATION IN NIGERIA

HEAD OFFICE: NIGERIA

HEATHROW HOUSE

HEATHROW CYBER SERVICES NIGERIA LTD

C/O 24 Kigoma Street,   Wuse Zone 7,   Abuja, FCT   Nigeria

Printed in Germany
by Amazon Distribution
GmbH, Leipzig